T5-CCL-840

GERALD R. FORD

a man in perspective

as portrayed in
The Gerald R. Ford Mural

by

[signature]

Photography by John R. Fulton Jr. and Candace Brown; Text by Tom LaBelle; Preface by Fred Myers; Design by Candace Brown; Poetry by W. Randolph Brown; Published by Wm. B. Eerdmans Publishing Company, Grand Rapids, Michigan.

Copyright © 1976 Paul Collins
All Rights Reserved
Printed in the United States of America
    by Hoekstra Printing Company, Grand Rapids

Credits

We publish this book with grateful acknowledgment to the Honorable Guy Vander Jagt, who sowed the first seed of the Gerald R. Ford Mural.

Our appreciation also goes to the Gerald R. Ford Mural Committee:

 Bobbie Butler, chairperson
 David Mehney, finance chairman
 Mrs. Hazel Grant
 Randolph Brown
 Burke E. Porter
 Yvonne Crump
 Rheta Collins
 Miss Arvilla Winegarden
 Miss Julia Tloczynski
 Tom Lee
 Cedric Ward
 Betty Tardy
 Paula Larson
 Miss Marcy Ulery
 Judge John Letts

We wish to credit Mr. Kenneth Thomasma for his research and help with this book.

And thanks to Eric Collins and Scott Collins for technical assistance.

Finally, special thanks to the following for their support and contributions to this project:

 Kawasaki Midwest
 Steelcase Foundation
 Grand Rapids Foundation
 Bethel Pentecostal Choir
 Grand Rapids Education Association
 Rapistan Foundation
 Fred Keller, Sr.
 Fred Keller, Jr.
 Mrs. Jimmy Van Atta
 Richard and Helen DeVos
 The Jefferson School Student Body
 Grand Rapids Public Museum
 Mr. and Mrs. Arthur Brown
 Sandra Eisert
 David Kennerly
 Billie Shaddix
 West Michigan Telecasters, Inc.
 WOTV
 Jack Hogan
 Lear-Siegler, Inc.
 Frederick G.H. Meijer
 Harvey Lemmen
 Kent County Aeronautics Board
 Peter C. Cook
 Robert Hooker
 Judas Brown

This book is dedicated to my mother,

Mrs. Rheta Collins,

who shared with me her spirit of

Independence and Perseverance.

Preface: The Mural

Mural painting is a most demanding kind of painting. A mural usually illustrates a specific idea or theme. This means that the mural painter does not have the luxury of ransacking the whole wide rich world (or the fascinating complexities of his own personality) for a pictorial theme that strikes his fancy. Instead he must work to program.

And he must think big. There are many square feet of blank wall to cover. These square feet have to be organized into a coherent whole while each part retains its own independent interest. In other words, the artist must allow for the fact that at some point onlookers will see the mural as a whole, responding to its total impact, while a moment later they will be looking at specific details of the composition, "reading" them for their meaning and resonances.

In his mural of Gerald R. Ford, artist Paul Collins has responded to the demands of the genre with vision and technical prowess. The mural has tremendous impact — the largest portrait head in it is 3½ feet high — yet the 32 separate images in the work are so clearly organized that they convey an enormous amount of information.

The Ford mural is not the first mural painted by Collins. Several others are in various locations in Grand Rapids, the most complete one, coincidentally, being in South Middle School, Gerald Ford's old high school. Then too, a good deal of Collins' early art work was in design and sign-painting with Randy Brown, Grand Rapids poet and commercial artist.

So Collins has had some experience with large-scale works. Nonetheless, the assignment was a staggering one. Make a painting 8 x 18 feet in dimension illustrating the life of Gerald R. Ford, a human being once a small boy like half the world's population, but a human being who grew into the most powerful position in the world.

Collins worked out a brilliantly direct way of making a pictorial composition of such a life. He placed front and center, very large and very close up, a portrait head of Ford as President. It shows Ford during a moment of introspection, pipe to his mouth. This particular image was developed by Collins from sketches he made during a work session on one of the President's visits to Vail, Colorado.

Ranging back into the mural from this monumental portrait are significant people and events in Ford's life. Their placement suggests that these may be the images in the President's mind during his moments of reflection. There are images of his wife and family as they look now, and there is a double portrait of Jerry and Betty when Ford was first elected to Congress.

Interestingly, these portrait heads are the only thing in the whole mural that Collins has done in color. What remains is simply drawing, a flexible yet disciplined network of black lines on a white background. The harmony between the black and white and the colored areas indicates that Collins works primarily in terms of value rather than hue, an honorable tradition — in fact the only tradition — in mural painting from the classical world through the Renaissance, and on up to the Mexican and WPA muralists of the 20th century. The lines of the drawing are the traces of a broad graphite pencil drawn across the regularly uneven surface of gessoed masonite panels.

The consistent texture of these pebbly grey lines melds together such differing images as Ford as an infant in his mother's arms, posing with his brothers, with a friend, hiking a football, dressed in his park ranger's uniform — images that include Ford's boyhood home, his first car, the Statue of Liberty, and the Presidential Seal. Some of these images are presented by the artist as old photographs, thereby emphasizing their role as the icons of a personal history.

Collins presents his compendium of images from a remarkable yet easily understood life with a well-honed instinct for the significant detail both in terms of connotation and technique. The mural has the effect of overall minute detail, yet careful observation shows that detailing is concentrated in certain passages — a hand, an eye, meticulously combed hair. The overwhelming truth of such passages convinces the observer of the verisimilitude of the whole; indeed, the super-clarity of the drawing suggests that the painting is realer than real. This convincing realism is undoubtedly the key to Collins' communication with his audience. His bravura technique commands appreciation from the untutored and the expert alike.

Easy to overlook is another Collins' forte that is equally important — his empathy with his subjects. The viewer feels that Collins relates strongly to the people he paints, from black people in Africa, to American Indians at Wounded Knee, to the President from Grand Rapids. He empathizes and is able to depict the essential humanity of each subject. He uses his impressive realistic technique to convey himself as an artist, yes, but more importantly to convey the essential qualities of the people he paints.

Fred Myers
Grand Rapids Art Museum

How
To encounter a symbol
And place him here
In the four sterile corners
Of this empty space
Touch him
Up close, touch him
Eyes will take the measure
And snatch a mug shot
For the history file
Of seldom men who held the reins

They are good eyes
They will feel the sinew beneath the cloth
Will gauge the heft and substance
Under surface things

Drink the voice
Roll it in your ears
Soak the flavor
Hold the resolute
And take it with you
Distill the entity
Take it with you

And with your fierce fingers
Place it in that cold blank space
And let him speak

Introduction

Shortly after noon on August 9, 1974, in a crowded East Room at the White House in Washington, D.C., Gerald Rudolph Ford of Grand Rapids, Michigan, was sworn in as the 38th President of the United States. He was the first President from Michigan, as he had been the first Michigan man to serve as Vice President.

The oath was administered by Chief Justice Warren Burger. The President-designate placed his hand on a Bible held by his wife Betty. It was opened to Proverbs 3:5-6: "Trust in the Lord with all thine heart; and lean not unto thine own understanding. In all thy ways acknowledge him, and he shall direct thy paths."

In a brief speech, the new President called on his countrymen to "restore the golden rule to our political processes and let brotherly love purge our hearts of suspicion and hate."

The nation knew little about him. For 25 years he had been U.S. Congressman from his home district. He was minority leader of the House of Representatives when he was chosen as Vice President by his predecessor in the White House, Richard M. Nixon. The 10 months in which he had served as Vice President were dominated in the news by scandal which eventually led to the resignation of President Nixon and Ford's ascension to the high office.

Gerald R. Ford appeared to be a man of uncommon integrity, a man with a deep commitment to openness and truth, a man who had opponents but no enemies. In the wake of the scandal which brought him to office, these were the qualities which seemed most important.

It was known that he was a hard, meticulous worker, and that he once had been an outstanding football player.

The nation also knew he was a man of family, with a beautiful wife, four bright and attractive children, and close ties with his brothers and other relatives back in Michigan.

He was a plain man. "I'm a Ford, not a Lincoln," he acknowledged in his first public utterance after his appointment as Vice President.

These qualities, homespun and homely as they may have seemed, but harking back to solid roots and a firm sense of self-identity, came as a relief to a nation grown distrustful of its institutions and leaders.

It is these qualities, and the people, events and associations which shaped them, which artist Paul Collins captures in his mural.

Jim Mencarelli

He was not yet Gerald R. Ford. Born July 14, 1913, in Omaha, Nebraska, he was named Leslie King Jr., son of a Montana wool dealer. His parents were divorced when he was two.

The Grand Rapids Press
Ford Becomes President
Takes Over Helm
Of Weary Nation
IN CONGRESS, JULY 4, 1776.
The unanimous
the thirteen united States of America
PRESIDENT OF THE UNITED STATES
©
July 1978

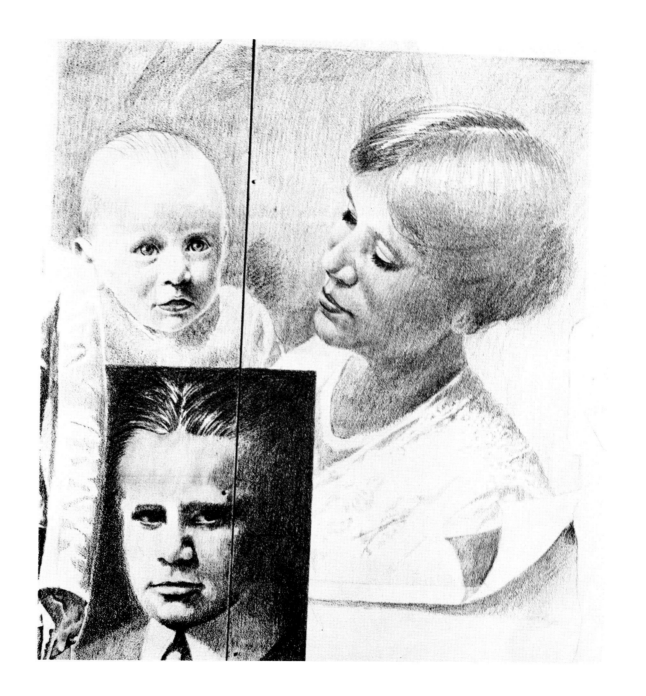

His mother was an attractive divorcee named Dorothy Gardner King. She had moved to Grand Rapids, and in 1916 she married Gerald R. Ford Sr., a young paint salesman. Ford adopted her son and renamed him Gerald R. Ford Jr., the first gesture in what was to be a warm, close relationship between the two men.

The future President was a healthy, well-loved baby who would have the privileges of an only child until he was five years old and the first of his three half-brothers was born.

Mother
Was always there
In the beginning
In the journey through the years
In the joy
The kisses and tenders
In the anger
In the strength
When the need came
To take a stand
In the love
In the pain
She was there always
In the boy
And the making of a man

Gerald R. Ford Sr. was the loving autocrat of a family of four sons. Besides Jerry, there were Tom, Dick and Jim. The elder Ford, a self-made man who never finished high school, was a firm disciplinarian who expected his boys to assume a full share of the household chores.

"He was my hero, my idol," President Ford would say of his father. The elder Ford opened a small paint factory in Grand Rapids in 1929 in partnership with another man. All the Ford sons worked in the factory at one time or other. The boys were instilled from the beginning with the values of hard work, truthfulness and independence, and were encouraged to get an education and rise in the world with honor.

A father is a hand to hold
Crossing the street
Or just walking
A yes, a no
A wordless smile
An angry look
Tone of scold
A warm fire
And constant table
A father is a strong thing
A hand at the helm
Is a rock
And discipline
Sometimes pain
Is a quick storm
Field of high wheat
Is a baker
When the world turns to
Bread left out in the rain

Growing up in Grand Rapids in the 1920s was a happy, active time for Jerry Ford, shown here with a boyhood buddy. Most of the boys in the neighborhood were bigger than he was, but he was husky and active and learned to keep up.

There always was a dog in the Ford family when Jerry was young. On one occasion the boys fixed up a cart in the form of a covered wagon, hitched up the dog and won first prize in a Boys Day Parade. Jerry is at left.

His teachers remember him as a conscientious if not brilliant student in grade school and high school (the picture is ninth grade), but in things which interested him strongly, like Boy Scouts or sports, he excelled.

Jerry Ford lost an election as class officer in high school, but he managed to make Student Council. He also was in the glee club, was captain of the football team, played second-string basketball and was on the track team.

He joined Boy Scout Troop 15 at Trinity Methodist Church and became an Eagle Scout with 35 merit badges. Later, as Vice President, he liked to point out to people that he was the first Eagle Scout to hold that office.

Ropes and boats
Sun, rain
Cold and snow
Trails, meadows
Fauna and forest
Bruises, badges
Pride and parades
Eagle scout, yes
Then

But from this side:
Only eaglet
Flexing the wings
To leave the nest
To test the hand
For the hunt
For the struggle
For the mate
And the flight
To the highest pinnacle
In the land

This drawing illustrates the first home the Fords lived in in Grand Rapids and Jerry's first car. There was never an abundance of money in the Ford family, but there usually was an automobile. Young Jerry Ford's first car was memorable mainly because of the way he lost it. It was an old Model T for which he paid $75 in his senior year in high school. The family had moved to East Grand Rapids, and Jerry needed the car to drive back and forth to South High School. (He had sought official permission to finish at South even though he then lived in another school district.) On a cold December day when he was just back from basketball practice, he put a blanket over the motor to keep it from freezing. The hot motor set the blanket on fire and the car burned spectacularly, and to a ruin. Jerry's father was sympathetic—until he found out Jerry had neglected to have the car insured. A very somber family dinner ensued.

Jerry Ford was an outstanding center at South High School in Grand Rapids and at the University of Michigan. "Thanks to my football experience," he would say later, "I know the value of team play. It is, I believe, one of the most important lessons to be learned and practiced in our lives." In his senior year at South, Ford was captain of the team which won the state championship. At Michigan he was named the team's most valuable player in his senior year and named to the Big Ten's All-Conference team. He was selected to play in the East-West Shrine Game and in the College All-Star Game against the Chicago Bears. But he turned down offers to play football professionally.

This wind on my sweat
It is good
It calls to things
In these quickened limbs
To excel
It is good
Always good to feel the juices
Calling to the best inside this flesh
I will reach down again
Low
To find the heights

In the summer of 1936, Jerry Ford served as a seasonal ranger at Yellowstone National Park, one of a myriad of jobs he held as a boy and young man. When he was in grade school, he sold magazines door to door. In high school he worked at a restaurant, was jack-of-all-work at Ramona amusement park on Reeds Lake and helped out at his father's paint factory. He washed dishes in a fraternity house at the University of Michigan, waited tables in the cafeteria of the university hospital and for a time was a professional blood donor, picking up $25 a pint once a month. At Yale he was assistant football coach and boxing coach.

Gerald Ford had graduated from Yale Law School and in 1941 had established a law practice in Grand Rapids when the Japanese bombed Pearl Harbor and brought the United States into World War II. He enlisted in the Navy April 20, 1942. He served first as a physical training officer, then—after his repeated requests—was given a combat assignment as assistant navigation officer on the small aircraft carrier Monterey. The Monterey saw hard action in the Third Fleet under Admiral William "Bull" Halsey in the South Pacific. But Ford's most dangerous moment came not against the Japanese but in a storm at sea in which he nearly was lost overboard.

Discharged from the Navy in 1946, Ford resumed his law practice in Grand Rapids and was courted by the county Republican organization to run as a "reform" candidate for U.S. Congressman. He agreed to run, but at the same time he was doing some courting of his own. The lovely Elizabeth Bloomer Warren had given up a budding career as a dancer in New York to return to Grand Rapids. She was fashion coordinator at a department store when she and Jerry began dating. They were married in October 1948— just after he had decisively beaten his opponent in the Republican primary, and just before he scored an even more impressive win over the Democratic candidate in the general election.

As a young congressman, Gerald R. Ford of Grand Rapids kept a low profile but observed and learned and quietly became expert in such things as military budgets. He built up a circle of trust and respect among his House colleagues. Meanwhile, he developed one of the finest systems of constituent service of any congressman. It didn't matter who had the problem among the people back home, young congressman Ford was an effective power in cutting red tape, solving difficulties and performing services. His helpfulness in major and minor constituent problems was regarded as his greatest strength in 12 elections to Congress in which he never received less than 60 per cent of the vote.

As mother to an active family of four children, Betty Ford was much in the background in her husband's early career in Washington. But as wife of the Vice President and later first lady, she blossomed in her own right. Her lack of pretension and her straightforward willingness to speak her mind bothered some but brought her admiration and liking from the great majority of Americans, particularly women.

Gerald Ford's lively family first came to notice in the Senate confirmation hearings when he was appointed Vice President. He revealed in testimony that he was able to buy a condominium at Vail, Colorado, for family skiing vacations because his children, avid skiers all, kicked in from their savings accounts—to be paid back later at regular interest. The children are Michael, born in 1951; John, born in 1953; Steven, born in 1954; and Susan, born in 1958.

It was Grand Rapids' proudest day when Gerald R. Ford became President on August 9, 1974, but the day was also profoundly disturbing. Two years of scandal had rocked the administration of President Richard M. Nixon, and had led first to the resignation of his Vice President and finally to Nixon's own resignation in the face of almost certain impeachment. In such an atmosphere, the ascension of Gerald R. Ford—who had been appointed by Nixon to replace the previous Vice President—was accompanied by vast national relief.

As President, Gerald Ford's first duty was to restore the dignity and respect of the highest office in the nation. It wasn't easy. As a means of putting the scandal irrevocably in the past, he pardoned President Nixon of any crimes which might be charged against him, then set resolutely to work on an inheritance of critical domestic and foreign problems. There was runaway inflation, mounting unemployment, a war in Vietnam which was coming to a frustrating and bitter end, and a shortage of fuel oil and other energy sources vital to the economy and lifestyle of the nation.

Gerald Ford went at this considerable agenda with his usual persistence and energy, bringing the war in Vietnam to a conclusion, setting in motion fiscal policies which helped avert what could have been a major recession and mounting an effective attack on the energy problem. Through it all, he established a style of honesty, candor and forthrightness which will be a model for presidents to come.